About the Author

Kris Bobosky is a single father of three grown children. His passion for writing began eight years ago and he continues to express himself through written word. He has written television sitcom scripts, a sci-fi novella and he has also been blogging since 2014. He is currently earning an Addictions Resource Worker diploma with an affinity to helping traumatized women in need.

Hearts Erased

Kris Bobosky

Hearts Erased

Olympia Publishers
London

www.olympiapublishers.com
OLYMPIA PAPERBACK EDITION

Copyright © Kris Bobosky 2022
Author photograph © Anya Mitchell

The right of Kris Bobosky to be identified as author of
this work has been asserted in accordance with sections 77 and 78
of the Copyright, Designs and Patents Act 1988.

All Rights Reserved

No reproduction, copy or transmission of this publication
may be made without written permission.
No paragraph of this publication may be reproduced,
copied or transmitted save with the written permission of the
publisher, or in accordance with the provisions
of the Copyright Act 1956 (as amended).

Any person who commits any unauthorised act in relation to
this publication may be liable to criminal
prosecution and civil claims for damage.

A CIP catalogue record for this title is
available from the British Library.

ISBN: 978-1-80074-852-1

This is a work of fiction.
Names, characters, places and incidents originate from the writer's
imagination. Any resemblance to actual persons, living or dead, is
purely coincidental.

First Published in 2022

Olympia Publishers
Tallis House
2 Tallis Street
London
EC4Y 0AB
Printed in Great Britain

Dedication

I dedicate this book to my children Jer, Lexis and Lindsey.

1

"The Face of Heaven"

No longer am I in your life
I think of your joy now and it saddens me.
In your presence you seemed so genuine
As though you cared a lot for me.
I grew so attached
You mesmerized me by the minute
You were why I returned each day.

I once confessed fragments
And you deemed me trouble.
You asserted I was drama
And that I displeased you greatly.
You crushed me
But my adoration still grew
Through my tears I cared even more.

Nothing could subside the throb
And I rode this wave for months.
For years you were the face of heaven
I knew I had to pull away. Apart.
But I kept dying a thousand deaths
All for another conversation with you.

You could do no wrong
While you cut my heart apart
So violently while you pretended to listen.
Ruthless and sadistic
Yet so beautiful to me
I can only blame myself.

My heart wanted you
And I should have sewn my lips shut.
I should have taken my blind love to the grave
Honesty set a trap and I sprung it more than once.
So, goodbye it is, it's healthier this way
Maybe one day I'll forget about you
The way you've already done the same.

You see, you've missed out royally
The way I felt for you moved mountains.
Rivers could vanish by my touch
I would have made you full
Full enough to burst but I couldn't make the walls fall down
I couldn't penetrate your center.

So, I guess I'm powerless after all
And the face of heaven will fade away.
I can now surrender my fight
Give up arms and leave this battle field for good.
None of this was real, none of it meant a thing
This whole time I was talking to myself.

2

"Bloodstained Hands"

Please excuse me while I kill you
Threads of brain with shreds of sinews.
Devastating lies continued
'til this silence swam within you.
Left alone to my devices
We find ourselves amidst this crisis.
Shattered skull is what the price is
Without tomorrow today is priceless.

Bide my time unto the grave
Your inner self I couldn't save.
By my mistakes this road is paved
To bloodstained hands, I am a slave.
I've tried my hardest and I've failed
Dwell in the dungeon where I'm jailed.
Seldom glimpse beyond the veil
Where's my heaven? This is hell.

Gutted and empty, the rug has been pulled
With fistfuls of anger my life's been annulled.
The system has failed me, 100% bull
No shield can protect you, you're worthless and null.

I'll slice and I'll slash and I'll carve you up nice
The blade will move fast on the canvas I dice.
Perforations and punctures not once and not twice
But repeatedly gory, the sum of what price?

To this seat I am banished
Everyone has but vanished.
Nothing good has been lavished
All I've known will be ravaged.
I alone to myself and myself deep inside
To recoil, to retract, on this day I must hide.
With my sins around my neck and my joy is denied
I have lived and I've died, there's no more to decide.

3

"Morning Comes Eternal"

We won't see the morning
On the road that we had tread.
Beat my fists against that wall
Over scrutinize my head.
Tethered to the unrelenting
Tethered to a thought within.
Not a destination or a place
I wanted to be in.
There was no one here to free me
To uncage me deep inside.
There was no new place to run to
There is no more place to hide.

In the shadows there is darkness
And in darkness there is light.
When the morning comes eternal
Face to face with the daylight.
In the blinding there is finding
Of the person inside me.
Because the person I'm becoming
Is whom I'm called to be.

So, this calibrated vision
Squandered no more in the night.
They have called me to obscurity
But I will choose to fight.
Keep my head above the waters
Cut the ties that held me back.
Do the work laid out before me
Must become my life's soundtrack.
Though the voices growl and whisper
Calling, nagging, mauling me.
This enlightened, titan version
Is the man I need to be.

In the shadows there is darkness
And in darkness there is light.
When the morning comes eternal
Face to face with the daylight.
In the blinding there is finding
Of the person inside me.
Because the person I'm becoming
Is whom I'm called to be.

This residuum of pain
Cursing my good Christian name.
Broken teeth and broken chains
There is no more of the same.
It is finished, it is done
I have traveled through the sun.
I am whole and I am one
Now the journeys just begun.

In the shadows there is darkness
And in darkness there is light.
When the morning comes eternal
Face to face with the daylight.
In the blinding there is finding
Of the person inside me.
Because the person I'm becoming
Is whom I'm called to be.

4

"In Her Castle"

In her castle she walks alone
Like a princess in a tower.
In control but of nothing
And with ease she stays away.
I saw her smile yesterday
Through the veil behind her window.
Though maybe I've lost my mind
In keeping up with the likes of her.
She keeps her furnace lit
And tosses in memories that make her feel.
Inside the flames to be removed
She will deny you like she did me.

In her castle she lives to die
Her perfect shell, shelved and off limits.
Yesterdays hurt is today's agenda
On repeat, in a loop.
Choking away present truths
And a lifetime of gifts at your feet.
Just open your eyes, simply see
But the formula won't allow it.
How I wished myself inside your bubble.

With you at the centre of your world.
All the ghosts and past mistakes
Equates who we are. Alone and together.

In her castle she withers slow
Soon there won't be anyone to find her.
In her beauty, so much magic
And in her magic, anesthesia.
One must walk a line to survive
But it's part of her waltz, premeditated.
I took large bites and begged for more
I ate what she offered for days, for months.
But there was no Oz behind the curtain
Because the curtain was a wall.
A thick, unpenetrated wall inside her castle
And none of us were allowed to breach.

In her castle the silence echoes triumphant
A victory cry where the winner took all.
Except what she took was our kindness
And our compassion complete.
See me, touch me. I am man
Broken yet moved. Interest unending.
This is how it is for a reason
Embrace it and cast the stalling aside.
Try me. Reply to me. Die for me. And I to you
To the governess of your life.
All control is not lost. There is no cost
Stand in the window and be exposed.

5

"To Be Loved by You"

To be loved by you
If I live long enough.
To see you unveiled
Consumes me in the now.
Extended invite into your world
On your sacred floors we dance.
Your eyes confess everything
Through my tears, I'm at your feet.
Servants heart
Now mending only in your courts.

To be loved by you
Quiets the storm in me.
Your walls destroyed
And in its place the lilies grow.
Time stood still
I can't stand the silence any more.
The radiance of a legion of angels
Permeates every pour.
Sometimes I have to look away
A beauty that leaves me blinded.

To be loved by you
Is it too much to ask?
Here we are but alone
You don't wonder where I've gone?
To be without your presence doesn't sit well
Exposed to the glorious goodness.
Then cast into darkness
Is a poison they made me drink.
Maybe I did it myself
But still there rides the longing.

To be loved by you
Is worth ten thousand tears.
The waiting breaks in daylights fall
Then carries on, it lingers long.
One moments kiss
Would seal your fate.
Inscribed in concrete and housed in diamond
The ground shakes under wild horses.
My love for you eclipses all
Unequivocal.

6

"Sanctify"

The pastel blues and crimson reds
In summer skies, hands behind my head.
You're with me now and nothing is wrong
I knew this all along.
Dodge the waves, water cold as ice
Inside this lake, outside the vice.
Cure me, blur me, dwell within
My bones forgive, inside my skin.
And on this grassy spot we lie
From all the distance you've implied
Forever eternal sanctify.

The yellows and orange, summer sunset disclose
Barefoot with you, water at our toes.
We built a fire stoked from within
You strike the match that burns in unison.
Your mouth is liquid sugar cane.
Kiss me deeply again and again
On whimpers breath of whispers left.
Amalgamate
The consummate.

Sanctify these limbs of mine
Let loose the arrows on the shrine.
I built from nothing inside my mind
Of you, to you, unknowing bride
Please sanctify me as I die.

I held your hand in August air
The faintest breeze caught in your hair
As time stood still, your eyes caught mine
You I consumed like blood red wine.
I spun you round, once then again
I dipped you, tripped you, stripped you down.
As one, I loved you evermore
Inside your nest, inside your store
Sanctified forevermore.

Kaleidoscope in summers bliss
This rainbow passion does exist.
Our bodies, spirits, minds are one
Engulfed in love and betrayed by none.
The shadows hide as we ride the tide
The waves, they crash with me by your side.
I promise you I've never lied
Inside, I'll die for you tonight
For you, my bride, the sanctified.

Sanctify these limbs of mine
Let loose the arrows on the shrine.
I built from nothing inside my mind
Of you, to you, unknowing bride
Please sanctify me as I die.

7

"Intruder Beware"

Fresh bleed
Deep cut
No one is listening
Open and glistening
The pooling of blood
Is an ocean deep squall
Its ripples eternal
An ethereal call.

Intruder beware
I know you don't care
I could spill out my story
But if not for your glory
And you pretend, you pretend
Phony ghost
You will perish.

Fall on my sword
In the daydreams cold sentence
This time there's no waking
I shall pay with your penance
On the snow

In the crimson
To be smothered in black
There is no coming back.

Intruder beware
I know you don't care
I could spill out my story
But if not for your glory
And you pretend, you pretend
Phony ghost
You will perish.

Boxed up
And served up
And all dialed in
Divine architect
Move us pawns from within
With life leaking out
One more laugh from your lips
As you shred my existence
Press delete and begin
Press delete and dig in
Press delete and you win.

Intruder beware
I know you don't care
I could spill out my story
But if not for your glory
And you pretend, you pretend
Phony ghost
You will perish.

You gut me and take away
Used up pieces on display
Forebode and forbidden
The lies you have hidden
In the quiet I bleed
In the darkness I'm freed
From the prison you're in
From the monster you've been.

Intruder beware
No, you don't effing care
I have spilled out my story
And for what? For your glory?
I bash you and crush you
Around your throat I must hush you
Phony ghost
You must perish.

8

"Beauty Incomprehensible"

Step out on a leaf
On a branch in the ocean.
We break free, you break me
And I can breathe on my own
Only to swallow your apprehension.
Gasping for air as I grasp a handful of your hair
Finally free, you bury the key
In your heart, in your skin.
Disallowing me in
Distanced by resistance
Shrouded in control.

Your fevered flesh
Keeps the blankets kicked aside.
It took your sickness to bring us back
Someplace cold we've never been
And the lights in your eyes terminate my demise.
I want inside, our souls collide
Something I've wanted so long.
Though I begged,
You wouldn't give in.
Now that you're mine,

It's divine, so divine.

Inches away, you might as well be air inside my coffin
I have to remind my hands not to touch you
And my lips not to kiss your skin in this room we're in.

You are beauty incomprehensible
A near obsolete radiance.
I shan't look away
My eyes eat you up
And demand more.
I'm a fool for you
A never learning tool.

All this and more
From behind this glass door.
You sat with me today, remember when I pounced?
Wasn't very pronounced, more so in my head.
Your hand did touch mine though
That much I recall
I melted in your recoil
It's never enough.
So, on and on it goes,
In the chapel of our commerce
Beneath the stage of acquiescence.

9

"Cinder"

Penciling lines under penicillin vines
Doing rewrite after rewrite
In the shadows of my mind.
Adding one to take away
You left a year ago today
"I don't love you any more" is the price I had to pay.
Filling time and killing wine
In the solace of our kind.
Undevoted to this crime
Underwater, undermined.

Though I lay my heart in hands apart
I'm torn in two, I'm bleeding you.
With veils aflame, sweet cinder glow
Please leave my head, let me let you go.

Things are different now
Than they used to be.
I've moved past me against you
To me versus me.
Back to where it began
Lost with my head in the sand.

I am free in this forest
Nothing left to deplore us.
Scattered sheep unto the killers
All these wolves craving innards.
With the lights all a-glow
In the sky down below.

Though I lay my heart in hands apart
I'm torn in two, I'm bleeding you.
With veils aflame, sweet cinder glow
Please exit my head, let me let you go.

Look in my eyes without the lies
We paralyze.
See past the trace of our disgrace
In your embrace.

I lay my heart in hands apart
I'm torn in two, I'm bleeding you.

10

"XYZ"

Her small hands in mine. In her room, waiting, still.

The touch of her skin. I am vapor.

Mingled the dust. Inhale.

A live possession. A bloodstream dive.

Hold my hand for we are eternal. Look at me, look to me.

No recourse. I can't fail you. Can you not see?

XYZ. Complete.

Branches in your sky. In the wind they sway.

Flourishing. Summer nourished.

And in you I am but away. For on your own you radiate.

Your song, up the back of my neck.

I watch from below. Exposed whilst hidden. My watery

eyes won't shut.

So, I wait, heart of wonder. Then it comes.

Autumn's stab. And you fall, from heights you plunge.

And I am there. I am here with arms to the sky.

And I will catch you. XYZ.

From dust to dust. Reborn though one, at least in my mind.

Everything becomes new, and I dwell in your world tonight.

But can you see me? Cut a vein, am I not there inside you?

Shapes twist into beating hearts and tempered libidos.

Was it him and her, or him versus the universe? I don't care for past tense.

We are here now… aren't we? My steps in circles.

With winters breath and silence illuminating. She is gone and she was never here.

And in the icy pool below is reflecting only you.

XYZ.

11

"Trinkets"

Intrepidly tripped up

Ripped out

Flip flopped and missing out.

Pie knuckle pissant

Gallantly gallivant.

Flight footed fairy-tailer

Underwater seahorse burial.

Corkscrew compass

Encompassing trumpets.

The now and the naysayers

Surveillant and flailing.

An eloquent elation

In this dark tribulation.

Stars, funnels and trinkets

Plinking placards delinquent.

Fully abashed with a cache

Full of passion.

She wrote of this densely

Immense and intensely.

With the licking and ticking

My wrist bomb keeps sticking.

Everything freezes

A treasonous bereaving.

We are numb, we are one

And we've lost to the sum.

But we're one, we are one.

12

"With Their Genitals Flailing"

With their genitals flailing
I took the cats sailing.
I floored it and quickly
Their nails in me prickly.
All they wanted was fish
On their teensy cat dish.
But I gave them a ride show
Little Whitney and Nigel.

So, we finally caught tuna
Off the coast of Bermuda.
And those cats had their fill
Then I gave them their bill.
Sitting pretty and anchored
Emailed funds from their banker.
Goodbye light, hello darkness
And then came my catharsis.

On the ocean with kittens
In my heart I'm so smitten.
With a lady on dry land
Yet I'm here in the wet sand.

Riding waves with these felines
Miles away from the moonshine.
On the bow doing crunches
Whilst my cats making lunches.

Stay afloat is the mission
Though I'm over here wishin'.
For an island adventure
Or some sort of redemption.
Though my cares, they avail me
These 2 cats remain blame free.
Back to life as remembered
All my dreams are dismembered.

So, I whittle a wood stick
On this sea of Saint Patrick.
Patron saint to the sinners
Eating bowls of Kraft Dinner.
With my cats in their doghouse
I look up to the lighthouse.
We are back, we're alive
None of this was contrived.

Drop the anchor and kiss me
Keep your government whisky.
I'm on land and I'm stable
I'm the head of the table.
Take the cats to the hen house
For their tuna was head loused.
Like a spank on the bare bum
This was one big conundrum.

13

"Little Font"

I don't have a photograph
Only memories
I've done the math, remained alone.
Now there is only me.
Not two of us, or her and he
On island sand you distanced me
A great divide, two canyons deep
In salty eyes so warm and sweet.

I don't have you here alone
I'm little font inside your phone.
The walls that keep you on your own
Are too the ones that cage me home.
Away from you
Contagious, too.
In black and white
Put down this fight.
I'm little font
Just little font.

Now time has passed and nothings changed
Arms length withstands

My adoration remains.
The night eternal, a vapors swirl
Pages away from boy gets girl.
Away from my thoughts
And everything's grand.
A grains worth of memory
And I'm sunk in your sand.
Betrayed by my longings
And coerced by my sight.
Please gouge out my eyes
If it takes all bloody night.

I don't have you here alone
I'm little font inside your phone.
The walls that keep you on your own
Are too the ones that cage me home.
Away from you
Contagious, too.
In black and white
Put down this fight.
I'm little font
Just little font.

The skeletons daydream
To have and to hold.
For flesh to inhabit
And blood that runs cold.
His heart must endure this
The spikes and the circling.
Now losing his breath
For his blood is now curdling.

One dose of her goodness
One stroke of the keys.
One heartfelt emotion
Bringing him to his knees.
Surely you miss this
Surely you're there.
Surely you care for me
Under all my despair.

I don't have you here alone
I'm little font inside your phone.
The walls that keep you on your own
Are too the ones that cage me home.
Away from you
Contagious, too.
In black and white
Put down this fight.
I'm little font
Just little font.

14

"Hair Down"

She's so beautiful
So, so beautiful.
There's not enough of her for me
I want it all, inside her soul.
Forever clawing at the surface
Open the door, please let me inside.
Been on this ledge too long
I refuse to jump.
Possess me further, I can't turn back
You've slit my guts
Now hold them tight.

Where is she now?
Is her hair down tonight?
Can I hear her voice?
Can this be our night?
I've felt this so long
Thought I made things right.
Can I tell her
I love you tonight?

Sometimes we end up where we need to be

I can't get loose of you and I've tried.
Melted to the floor, immovable, indisputable
Transfusable, and reusable.
A simple greeting and I'm high all day
You impact me thoroughly.
To me you matter. You matter most.
And the madder I make you
Will never break you.

There she is
Her hair across her shoulders.
Speak to me
Make tonight the night.
Do you see my glow?
Can we take this step?
You need to know
I love you so
I love you so.

Let me eat your heart
And hold your soul.
Swim in your blood
And mend the holes.
Let down your wall
So, you can bleed in me.
Don't look back now.
Just be with me.

There she is
So, so beautiful.
Is her hair down tonight?

15

"I Will Hold You Up If You Hold My Hand"

This life, what a world, such a fabulous mess
Do we die? Do we choose to succeed at our best?
In the lines and the layers of this cosmic BS
Flickers moonbeams aligning what was once to regress.
I do love you, it's true, I don't care if it's odd
Shining light in the dark to unmask the facade.
Just take my hand, I will lead and you follow
Close your eyes, take a breath, I just want you to know.

Inside that house there's a place for me
And beside myself could be you with me.
And under that roof and between those walls
Lives a love we've never known at all.
This could be our thing, this could be our call
Instead of falling down we can both stand tall.
I will hold you up if you hold my hand
In this home of ours we could have never planned.

I never wanted my heart to be filled
So much when I'm near you, I'm empty, it spilled.

It's nothing you do and it's not what you say
But everything else just blurs all away.
The clutter, the chaos, the bills and the nonsense
Flush it all down, wipe away our subconscious.
I'm pleading you, bleeding you, imperfectly saying
I could love you forever, so deeply, I'm praying.

Inside that house there's a place for me
And beside myself could be you with me.
And under that roof and between those walls
Lives a love we've never known at all.
This could be our thing, this could be our call
Instead of falling down we can both stand tall.
I will hold you up if you hold my hand
In this home of ours we could have never planned.

16

"The Wall Inside Her Garden"

There's a wall inside her garden

Within dreams it hides her face.

And the moment she is with me

Is the moment it's erased.

She is trying to forget me.

In her mouth, that sour taste.

And she's bleeding good intentions

This is only just a phase.

In her garden there's a light on

Up where she can only see.

From behind this wall of silence

She is looking out for me.

But she's blocked me from her vision

Now she can't communicate.

So I sit and pray, the only way

The proper way to wait.

There's a wall inside her garden

And it thickens by the day.

Vegetation vines are choking

Her emotions, they betray.

There is something to return to

Should the stubborn die in vain.

There is love forever after

Right here in the driving rain.

There's a wall inside her garden.

For my crimes there is no pardon.

It appears her heart has hardened.

In the wall inside her garden.

17

"My Favorite Mess"

With this knife I carved your flesh. Elbow deep in blood red mess.

Your lungs collapse and sinews burst. I've not yet hungered for this thirst.

The life you lose becomes one I gain. I've become addicted to this pain.

A haunting zeal, metamorphic change. Fully composed, I'm not deranged.

Your silence breeds where loss is found. Your quiet screams deep underground.

Sarcophagus all furnished now, for visitors from out of town.

You didn't count, you weren't of use. This retribution was your noose.

In somber thoughts, I reinvent. I'll not forget your sweet,

sweet scent.

The days remind, the nights confess. You'll always be my favorite mess. The past alive, the present waits. My thoughts of you, they constipate. Forever present my disdain. Intertwined we can't relate. My thoughts of you, they constipate.

All in vain and all in waste. I vandalized and killed in haste.

Your funny laugh will be no more. I stomped it hard into the floor.

You've been erased, you never were. You weren't my she, you weren't my her.

It's pissed away and will not be. At least I have my sanity.

The days remind, the nights confess. You'll always be my favorite mess. The past alive, the present waits. My thoughts of you, they constipate. Forever present my disdain. Intertwined we can't relate. My thoughts of you, they constipate.

Knock knock? It's you beyond the grave! You're clawing back. You're saving face!

Knock knock? It's you, invading me! Degrading me. Persuading me!

Knock knock? It's you, that voice prevails! You call to me.

You call from hell!

Knock knock? It's you, you don't exist! So stay away you septic cyst!

The days remind, the nights confess. You'll always be my favorite mess. The past alive, the present waits. My thoughts of you, they constipate. Forever present my disdain. Intertwined we can't relate. My thoughts of you, they constipate.

18

"He Kissed The Backs Of Her Hands"

He kissed the backs of her hands, for they held his world.

He put his face in her palms, and she healed his soul.

He placed his lips on her forehead, and the heavens did shake.

He took her face in his hands, and her spirit came awake.

He kissed the backs of her hands, when her promises she broke.

He put his face in her palms, each time the relationship would choke.

He placed his lips on her forehead, when the money was gone.

He took her face in his hands, as his heart cried this song.

He kissed the backs of her hands, as she died in his arms.

He put his face in her palms, when she wished him pure harm.

He placed his lips on her forehead, as she spread her disease.

He took her face in his hands, while she brought him to his knees.

He kissed the backs of her hands, in his dreams, all alone.

He put his face in her palms, although blocked on her phone.

He placed his lips on her forehead, With the gun to his own.

He took her face in his hands, as the trigger was pulled.

He kissed the backs of her hands, as his body lay silent.

He put his face in her palms, left a scene, oh, so violent.

He placed his lips on her forehead, now cold, without feeling.

He took her face in his hands, as his soul left the ceiling.

19

"Trails Of Iniquity"

We are all aborted
Nothing to regret
Never had a chance
Never will advance
We are all aborted.

Cast into a world of sin
Crawling backwards from within
Orphaned, fatherless
Penniless, hopeless
Tossed aside and left to die
Blind eye turned to the empty urn
I will arise, I will arise!

Born dead and unfed
Umbilically, symbolically
Abandoned, exiled
Hated, crushed
Thrown asunder, lacking all
Without ears to hear the call
I will arise, I will arise!

We are all aborted
Nothing to regret
Never had a chance
Never will advance
We are all aborted.

I'll take it back
I'll change it all
My purpose here is not to fall
I won't stay dead
I will prevail
So what if he wants me to fail
He cannot win
He knows he's lost
The price is nothing worth the cost
I'm on my feet
I won't stay down
From Satan I take back my crown.

We are all aborted
Nothing to regret
Never had a chance
Never will advance
We are all aborted.

20

"Magnet Of The Unsound"

Darkness, decay
Malevolent gray
Dawn fast forwards to night.
Kill with kindness
Eternal blindness
Never asking for a fight.

Let the damaged come to me
Maybe all there'll ever be.

Blistered triumph
Joy now fleeting
Indecisive and defeating.
Pushed away
Rejection searing
Attraction's faceless love endearing.
True confusion
Brought to surface
Convalescing without purpose.
Bash my brains
And gouge my spirit
Ripping, licking pain, endure it.

Let the damaged come to me
Maybe all there'll ever be.

Dartboard heart
Just fire away, the pin hole wounds
Rot on display.

Gash me, splash me
Paint in blood
Deceptive pleasure from above.
Ruptured, bleeding
Foolish needing
Choose the broken, always leading.
In the darkness, I will fester
Lies, they're yelling
Death sequestered.

And let the damaged come to me
Maybe all there'll ever be.

I will fix them, I will save them
I can fix you, I can save you.
I will fix them, I will save them
I can fix you, I can save you.

Let them come to me
All I ever see
Broken, jig sawed, headless, lifeless
Let them come, for I am eyeless.

Let the damaged come to me
Maybe all there'll ever be.

21

"Hearts Erased"

Here we are, apart again

Miss all those little things.

And where we were, was not the same

As we once had been.

Days like sand, they go away

Hand in hand yesterday.

And so, we are alive again

But why can't I breathe you in?

We live our lives as enemies

Why must it be like this?

When once we had no walls between

The day of our first kiss.

Our hearts are healed, made room for more

The canvas is erased.

Still looking at our lengthy thread

Oh, what I'd give just for a taste.

Reach for me

Just one more time.

Without the pain

With hearts erased.

Breathe in me

No more killing time.

It can be the same

With hearts erased.

I started fresh, some random girl

Her name it still eludes me.

I called her you when the kissing grew

And now she's jumped into the sea.

Her death, I know, should mean something

But I don't want to fight it.

Because what I feel for you tonight

Trumps all, I'm undivided.

Reach for me

Just one more time.

Without the pain

With hearts erased.

Breathe in me

No more killing time.

It can be the same

With hearts erased.

I dated you.

I hated you.

I love you so.

Please don't let go.

You tasted me.

You wasted me.

I love you so.

Please don't let go.

Reach for me

Just one more time.

Endure the pain

With hearts erased.

Breathe in me

No more killing time.

It can't be the same

With hearts erased.

22

"Light Eternal"

Sitting
Hemming
Hawing
Breathing deeply.
Touching
Feeling
Crawling slowly.
Heaving
Healing
Coming forward.
Inching upward
To the
Ceiling
Glowing
Throbbing
Spewing reason.
In the
Garden
Of my
Demons.
Fully wakened
Naked

Lonely.
Vision
Shining
Round the
Center
Of my
Being
Is electric.
Sinews
Tangent.
Surface renders
Light eternal
Spotlight splendor.

23

"Wanderings"

Rose petal lips

Soft kiss eternal

Bleed in me

Intoxicants flush

Your perfume negates all rational thought.

The clink of the glass

With my hand on your ass.

Delusions infusion

Of wanton cravings

And other such lusting's

Drowning insolvent.

The appeal is illusion

Bombastic collusion.

On an island and dying

Life itself is unwinding.

Trapped inside terrifying

Common sense I'm defying.

Insidiously plunging

A part of me.

Suffice it to say

We wished it away.

So that's where it lay

In eternal decay.

24

"The Descent"

Ethereal, immortal
A guilty pleasure.
Radiance imbibed
Raw and docile
Made new, undulating
Ripened anew
A glorious uprising
Luminous
Unfettered
And divine.

But those voices
Whisper low sweeping murmurs
Soothing blasphemous
Venomous vibrations
Bathed in black
She stares
The mirror swimming
Abhorrent glares
While the echoes chant horror
High the tides come to swallow.

Never to return
Fragile innocence
Violated violently
The pillages requiem
On loop eternal
Where once beauty bred
Aborted gestation
Renderer of misfortune
And the downfall of your Eden
Behold, and bow down.

25

"Incandescence"

Her silhouette is all she ever had

Mosaic existence in caricature locale.

Dreaming vibrant illusions

Tear-stained pillow her canvas.

Living life without title

Indiscriminate and alone.

Her shadow is blinding

Her backstory rewinds

Reset and resentful.

What do they know?

What does she care?

Because when the glow comes

She is lifted high.

When the glow comes

Those morphine eyes.

Incandescent.

Incandescence.

Immortal and distorted

Creeps a smile and burns the portrait.

Procrastination euthanized

Incoherent way of life.

The puzzle pieces crumble and break

Make no mistake.

Rudderless

Emptied vessel thirsting, bleeding.

Sins replenish as she's kneeling

A new found faith, just one step taken.

Shut them out

As she awakens.

Because when the glow comes

She elicits power.

When the glow comes

In this final hour.

Incandescent.

Incandescence.

Redeemed catharsis

Purged and healing.

Sewn together

In this season.

Reveal the knife

The gleam of silver.

What doesn't give strength

Just might kill her.

Slit their throats

One by one.

Splashing color

Behind the sun.

Because when the glow comes

Tomorrow becomes today.

When the glow comes

With you she'll have her way.

Incandescent.

Incandescence.

26

"Mezzanine"

She's so beautiful

Tussled and dreamlike

Her hair spins in the winds

As the pins in my shins relocate

To my heart, pruned and hung

Beaten more than beating.

She's so perfect

A touch of radiance divine

Morning mist, moon kissed

Freelance lovers

Of once upon a fantasy.

Let loose gravity

Flung to the corners

She was everything

And I am without her.

Pouting and doubting.

Conception through death

Bits and particles

Puzzle dispersed

A play we once rehearsed.

She is immortal

Genesis without end

Web is spun and neither won.

I shan't forget

The ashen brunette

Melting memories splash and wade

Nothing darkens

Nothing fades.

27

"She Walks Alone"

Never a moment duller than this
She's out and about and her plan is to kiss the first charming suitor with skills to recruit her
Her heart is the bullseye and he's a sharpshooter.

But I'm thinking thoughts, the ones reasonably stated
That conjure up sadness and keep me frustrated
I want her to be here, to listen and show me outside of the worries without sugar coating.

My hearts gonna burn, gonna pop, gonna sizzle
I leave it exposed and it always delivers the good with the wretched and sick with the normal
I can't feel my feelings, so I won't feel my sorrow.

The plentiful longings, the yearns and the aching's are hers for the owning, they're hers for the taking
Wallowed abysmal with thoughts cataclysmal
Please reach for me, preach to me
Breach the black dismal.

Her world condescends the transcendent uprising
She's minutes away yet I'm here and I'm writhing
Can't stay in the past or reside in the future
I tumble and stumble in my present stupor.

Down here on my knees with the keys to her heart
Does she know I exist? Let's go back to the start
To revive it again, we can thrive in the end
Because we lived and we died, hand in hand we ascend.

28

"Dishonesty"

Where have you gone?
The reflection denies
While I sit and I ponder and meet my demise.
I'm lonely and bleeding
So alone under earth
You've forgotten my name, feel abandoned since birth.
Gutted, rebutted, rebuked and declawed
A fraction, a figment, no powerful Oz.
Dissolving and dying, there's no point in trying to come to my rescue so please stay in hiding.

Where did you go?
Why do you hide?
Embedded and masked and bloody contrived.
Your thoughts void of feelings
And feelings of thoughts
This incarceration, my spirit is bleeding.

I was a lie, did I ever exist?
There's nothing to show from a slice to the wrist.
I'm vomited matter, rejectable splatter
Unseen and unwanted, transparently flaunted.

By a snap of your fingers, my soul it doth linger
In stages I bury this consummate wringer.
My leprous detachment of all that is sterling
Dead on arrival and rancid and burning.

Where did you go?
Why do you hide?
Embedded and masked and bloody contrived.
Your thoughts void of feelings
And feelings of thoughts
This incarceration, my spirit is bleeding.

Find me
Atone me
Baptize and dethrone me.
Stitch my flesh, sealed and clean
Reveal who I now shall be.
Teach me your vengeance, please
Then bury my one disease.

Dishonesty
Nail this to your tree.
Dishonesty
Kill it with me.

29

"Six Feet"

You brought me here to drown
I am six feet under now.
Your hands, they held me tight
Then they opened up tonight.

I loved you without question
Followed heart and soul and mind.

Swallowed up by mercy
Felt like only God's design.

But I walked into a trap
A simple bait and switch routine.

Where what I wanted was rescinded
Then you handed me my spleen.

You broke it all, there's no way back
You put it on another's back.
You broke it all and I resent you
Matters not what's your intention.

You brought me here to drown
I am six feet under now.
Your hands, they held me tight
Then they opened up tonight.

It was just a dream, then you woke me
With a pillow, you did choke me.

I'm awake now, I can see
I guess I need a lobotomy.

Cause I need to walk away
I need to love again one day.

It's all tragic and disgusting
But I can't lay here simply rusting.

You broke it all, I can't believe
Both you and I you both deceive.
You broke it all, it's still surreal
I used up all the way I feel.

You brought me here to drown
I am six feet under now.
Your hands, they held me tight
Then they opened up tonight.

30

"She's Enough"

My eyes had bled without your grace
Undying witness to a life unquenched.
I was not informed of the plan
The sights I'd see and the killing I've done.

The things I am capable almost all came true
Never knowing I would end up right here with you.
And in the end of our beginning
My life begins and ends with you.

I was always someone else, meaning better but not quite there
Half man, half demon, all hurting.
The swirls of dissatisfaction encased me
Imprisoned by my own hand.

I never thought about you, also suffering in your own loss of plight
I never considered what monumental insanity you were apart of
And I'm sorry I didn't know.
For I would have slain your giants for you.

I would have killed them all for you
Broken necks and no good cheques.
The times of loss, though wrong the love
I would have held you, bracing war.

Down in a hole, up to your throat
Those times you barely stay afloat.
Where was I to leave you be?
Shouldn't I have always taken lead?

It must be true that there was no other way
My heart is there but if I had saved you all those times
You wouldn't be who I fell in love with today.
I would be disallowed the knowledge of you now and that would break my heart.

I love you, do you see this?
No matter what brought us here, we are here, now, together.
So, we embrace the quiet for this is earned
You and I. Nothing else matters.

31

"Rejection"

His heart, now raw and bleeding
The tears, they make him blind.
In shadows wrought with abandonment
This darkness he doth find.

The sadness, it surrounds him
Wash like waves on rippled earth.
Didn't see this hammer falling
Always wanted a rebirth.

Screaming at his maker
Questions falling to the floor.
All he's done means nothing
And it will forever more.

Splintered hope decimates
Let the cold of winter bury.
Lying naked on frozen ground
Numb to nature's fury.

Embalmed in ice, no longer feeling
Eyes frozen open, no longer dealing.

The weight removed but betrayal, it festers
This twisting knife, a life molester.

And all is still and all is silent
The pain is gone in death compliant.
Where love was promised, now burnt black
Just empty nothing echoes back.

32

"Where Failure Breeds"

Look in these eyes and don't look away
Deaf maybe dumb but irrelevant today.
I claw at you, digging in, holding on tight
In a matter of minutes, I've sunk in my bite.

Feeding and gnawing and burrowing in
I am now inside you, aligning your sin.
Allotting you sickness, indwelled in your chest
Twisting and turning, embrace your death.

Let the waters refresh and drown
The river will take me down.
And if I float back to the surface
Replenishment, baptized, refurbish.

Alive indeed
Let me bleed.
On the host I feed
Where failure breeds.

The illness is spawning, you're no longer you.
Invisible toxin swims its way through.

On permanent bed rest with walls closing in
This cancerous prison breathes horror within.

Your ears now they burn for you shouldn't have listened
The pain is too much in this living abyss and
Everything pulsates and every cell dies
If only you hadn't believed all those lies.

Let the waters refresh and drown
The river will take me down.
And when I float back to the top
You'll never flee, I'll never stop.

Alive indeed
Let me bleed.
On the host I feed
Where failure breeds.

Haunted screaming paralysis
The cycle now complete.
Chains hang heavy, anchor embedded
Buried and replete.

33

"Your Pulsing Aorta"

You were as discreet as I was sweet
A thimbleful of self-doubt
In a backdrop of half confessions
None of which resonated with you.
You didn't absorb the way I did
Though I would have spent all day by your side and in your mind.
Amidst your sheets, so heavenly
My missteps and pratfalls
Elevated by your hourly rebukes
I didn't wrong you though neither did I impress nor digress.
My heart was your piñata
All the good stuffed inside
You must have burst it over a hundred times.
I taped it so poorly
Knowing another shatter was inevitable.
I brandished the rod
And readied it in your little palms.
Wincing, I closed my eyes
Bracing for the welcome pain because it came, oh, it came so good.

I've been discarded before
If it doesn't concern you, I should remove myself.
Your dirty work is done
The blood is on my hands
My tent pitched in no mans land
Away from you but closer too.
Face to face with your pulsing aorta
The ventricles amuse me.
In your blood I want to stay
To take up residency and build my own community within.
Nothing can stop your beauty from bombarding me
Like a plate of peeled potatoes
Welt inflicting if I don't receive it right.
I must take ease in everything you
For it all screams your name
Hurled at me each step, every day.
I am neither inside you nor am I dead and it all feels glorious.
Waves, they waft and billow so
You're locked inside. I won't let go.

34

"You Are Euphoria"

Her eyes are pools
With depths unknown.
A stones throw ripples
Like a thousand echoes.
She radiates glory
And commands my affection.
With dividends of worship
To her I am immortal entwined.

Our hearts drip with inclination
As we reside amongst desire.
The heady, slick intoxicant
Buries and teeters me constant.
Since you are the light
Then set me a glow.
Smolder the wick
And engulf us consummate.

My adoration for you is legion.
You're better off counting the stars.
Our crossroads enigma dwarfs even the most sensible of us.
I don't know what love died to grant us ours but if I could

thank them I would.
I can't withstand the weight of your love.
It bends. Overpowers. I'm down on my knees.

And in the midst of our triumph
There is grand tragedy.
An accolade that befalls us
Subservient to the prevailing rapture we emersed ourselves in.
My zeal for you cannot be untied.
Nor tainted at the gravest of costs.
Through the burning tears
Nothing is lost and with everything to gain.

We cannot be burdened with mortality.
Our love is of invincible nature.
And no one holds cause against
What we swore we would never relinquish.
What can't be taken will only flourish beyond our wildest imaginations.
Therefore, we must inhabit this enamored state.
Dissatisfaction lies dormant in this keyhole Eden of which we've only read about.

So, under a name new we advance wholeheartedly.
We walk as one under the sun.
You are euphoria. Untouched and novel.
You are my healer and I, your keeper.
Defender and servant.
And in the face of death there is life.
One that will never cease.
And you and I will remain unscorched.

35

"Love Illicit"

Your head nestled in the hollow of my neck
Inside our cave of satisfaction.
Contentment of a thousand wishes
Exploring the surface of my platitude.
The unknowingness removed
Leaving slivers of comfort for days.

You are so worthy
And are embedded in my flesh.
Skewered showers
Makes for an imperfect cleansing.
A baptism designed for the joining of our souls.

Unite these hearts
As the venom creeps within. Poison is unable to conquer love
But with blood inflamed, we liquify.
Vaporized and into the fray we go.

Untouchable in the fire
And our desire only grows.
We are fasting loneliness in these moments of rapture.

Immortal, we ascend
Til death envelopes the dust we are.

Those years we had on earth transcend
Since our ascent, all is made new.
We are light years from the pain of separation
No more moments fixed on failures
And with nothing to regret.

Swim with me through the cosmos
We are floating galactic.
I breathe your air
And the sinews of my soul align in you.
We are here, touched by light
Transfixed eternal.

You hold the key to my intoxication
The idea of you remedies me whole.
Where others delivered death without passion, you erupt adoration for days.

I am sewn into the pocket of your kindness
I am inside you as you reside amidst me.
Your secrets I imbibe while I drink from your naked waters.
Our love illicit radiates. Illuminates.

Where roads have lost the only way
I'm kneeling here with lips to your feet.
To serve
To be among loves embrace.